GEORGE GERSHWIN®
THE ANNOTATED

Rhapsody In Blue™

RESTORED TO GERSHWIN'S ORIGINAL MANUSCRIPT BY
ALICIA ZIZZO

D1737684

FOREWORD
By Alicia Zizzo

Few composers have written material that has been more improvised upon, imitated, fragmented and generally misinterpreted than George Gershwin's. And at the top of "most defiled" is the *Rhapsody in Blue,* which, ironically, is the very composition that defined for the classical community for the past seventy years who George Gershwin is. In the most recent edition of Schirmer's *Manual of Musical Terms,* Theodore Baker refers to Gershwin as a great American songwriter and composer of jazz-flavored "serious" (facetiously quoted by Baker) works. Even the *New Grove Dictionary* finds his serious compositions "structurally defective . . . filled with repetitive rather than developed melodies" often "separated by abrupt pauses." These particularly negative assessments are not wrong—if one studies and judges the originally published *Rhapsody in Blue* for piano solo and the *Rhapsody in Blue* for piano and orchestra published for two piano/four hands in 1924. What makes these critically devastating assessments so poignantly tragic is the fact that Gershwin's judges were condemning flawed editing, not flawed composing.

A twist of fate and Gershwin's lack of participation in the original publication of the *Rhapsody in Blue* led to an unanticipated altered composition that was shrouded in unanswered questions for more than half a century. To begin with, Gershwin's *Rhapsody in Blue* has not been in the public domain, which would have yielded access to his original manuscripts. Additionally, Harms Publishing Co., which in 1924 was not in the business of issuing classical music scores, specialized in popular songs and musical theater geared to the great mass of amateur pianists in that era of player pianos and silent movies. The editors at Harms who had been assigned the task of preparing the *Rhapsody* for publication were classically trained musicians who had been educated in the European traditions that had produced Tschaikowsky and Rachmaninoff. They neither understood Gershwin's style nor did they have any great respect for his lack of conservatory training. They ultimately determined to edit the *Rhapsody* according to their views on how the piece should be performed. First they deemed it too long. In the piano/orchestra edition, they deleted more than fifty measures in the piano solo part and cut out four measures in the orchestra. My unanswered query has long been: "Why so much in the piano and so little in the orchestra?" In the piano solo edition of the *Rhapsody*, eighty-eight measures were eliminated from the original manuscript in Gershwin's hand! Small wonder it was considered fragmented and truncated. The melodies "separated by abrupt pauses" did not exist in Gershwin's manuscript. Beautiful bridges connecting thematic material had been cut in half. Passages that originally were written as an ascent followed by a descent were now simply a descent found somewhere in another register, totally unconnected to what preceded it. In one section, twenty piano solo measures leading to the entrance of the lush final theme were reduced to ten. There is another sixteen-measure section most egregiously and unjustifiably cut out just before the finale of the piece. In fact, none of the deletions can be justified because they reflect irresponsible musicianship.

In addition to shortening the *Rhapsody* by approximately four or five minutes, its editors also brought their own pedagogical style to it. That is to say, they altered Gershwin's own verbal and interpretive directives to the extent that the performance of the piece went from lighthearted and jazzy to heavy-handed and romantic in the style of the nineteenth century. This is what these turn-of-the-century editors knew, and this was the style of piano playing that was being taught to students and performers. Ultimately, this became the style pianists have been bringing to the *Rhapsody* to this day. But this is not the style one finds notated in Gershwin's hand.

If Gershwin had personally directed these changes, there would exist proof somewhere. None has been found. We do know that Gershwin gave his blessing to the original publications. He was, in fact, surprised that Harms would have published it at all. We also know that he had expressed his desire to talk to his publishers about the changes sometime in 1993, but never followed up.

What we do have, however, is absolute proof that Gershwin performed his *Rhapsody* February 12, 1924, as he had originally notated it in his own hand. Two manuscripts exist: the first in Gershwin's hand and the second which is Grofe's orchestrated manuscript. Both scores are identical. Grofe did not alter a single note, chord or any other directive of Gershwin's. Accordingly, Gershwin continued to perform the *Rhapsody* as he had originally notated it. He also performed it as it had been published. He recorded a nine-minute *Rhapsody* in 1927 and a short piano solo *Rhapsody* on piano rolls. Gershwin's adaptability and huge public success no doubt irked some of his contemporaries, which only fired the myth that he was less than masterful as a composer.

Another extension of the myths surrounding Gershwin's genius has to do with the notion that he had not experienced any real evolutionary process that led to the composition of the *Rhapsody*. Actually, this piece had very definite roots in a major work he had composed in 1922 titled *Blue Monday*.* A twenty-minute opera combining Impressionist and Romantic styles with jazz motifs, it yields a fine insight into his command of harmony and music history. Paul Whiteman had conducted *Blue Monday* for George White's *Scandals* and was impressed enough to invite Gershwin to compose something similar for his "Experiment in Modern Music" concert at Aeolian Hall in New York. Rushed to produce a major work for Whiteman, Gershwin dug into his memory (consciously or not) and referred to *Blue Monday* for this endeavor. He decided upon the rhapsody as a form (a Greek word that, ironically in view of the fate of the *Rhapsody*, means "to sew together" various musical themes). As it turned out, the seams holding his thematic material together were the very same used by his original editors to cut and unravel the *Rhapsody*. To add insult to injury, when the *Rhapsody* for piano solo was created by Harms, rather than consulting the original Gershwin manuscript, most of the orchestral reductions for second piano were used instead.

It is also of interest to note that the second part of the first theme of the *Rhapsody*, which is also used as its ending, is the same as the ending of *Blue Monday* and can be found for the first time in *Lullaby* (Warner Bros. Publications), a piano piece written in 1919. It later evolves into *The Man I Love,* written in 1927.

In this present edition, the first new edition in more than seventy years, all previously deleted passages are reinserted and, with the exception of four measures, appear in both the original Gershwin piano manuscript and the original Grofe orchestrated manuscript. Also included here are all slurs, written instructions, staccato markings, pedaling, chords and other interpretive directives given by Gershwin in his own hand. There was virtually no page in his manuscript that had not been altered in some way. Total corrections number in the hundreds and have been footnoted as much as possible in the solo piano version and in the addendum to the orchestra/piano edition.

Where Gershwin left blanks and incomplete notation, or where the complex voicings are impossible to play in a two-hand version, editorial intervention was necessary. All editorial work has been done after extensive research to ensure authenticity and is intended to suggest to performers what they must ultimately determine for themselves.

Musicological history has been made with this new edition, for it will afford future generations far removed from current memory a frame of reference to one of the world's outstanding musical figures. George Gershwin has finally taken his well-earned place among the great composers of the nineteenth and twentieth centuries. The myths surrounding the *Rhapsody in Blue* are now dispelled.

Blue Monday, arr. for piano solo from Gershwin's original ms. by Alicia Zizzo; WARNER BROS. PUBLICATIONS

ACKNOWLEDGMENTS:

To my steadfast friend and advisor, Edward Jablonski, I owe immeasurable gratitude and admiration for his infinite store of knowledge. To the Gershwin family, friends and kindred souls; my hope is that I have fulfilled their wishes.

To Tony Esposito, Product Line Manager, Warner Bros. Publications, whose energy and understanding of the real Gershwin allowed this project to proceed.

To Avraham Sternklar, a powerful composer, who reinforced my will to see this Herculean task come to a conclusion.

Rhapsody in Blue for Piano and Orchestra:
Corrections and Restorations According to the Original Manuscript in Gershwin's Hand
Dated January 7, 1924
(The only markings included here are Gershwin's unless otherwise noted)

Researched, restored, and edited by Alicia Zizzo

Addendum – 1

PAGE 3

Bar 1: Note repeated A♭.
f is only dynamic given.
Note staccato over C♭, followed by portamento.

Bar 3: Note changes in second chord.

Bars 4–5: Fourth chord is not tied. They are written as sixteenth notes with (♪) rests in between:

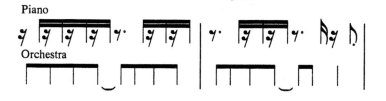

Bars 6–11: Note different phrasing.
"rit." is only tempo given in Bar 10.
Note E♮ octave in bass.
The word "Chord" is written but not notated in Bar 10.

Bar 9 (Page 3) and Bars 1–2 (Page 4): No "tenuto" is indicated in original manuscript.

4

PAGE 4

Bar 7: "Poco rall." not indicated.
Martellato not indicated in Bar 3.

Bars 9 and 10: No ⟨ ⟩ indicated.
Also no ⟨ ⟩ on Page 5 Bars 4 and 5.

PAGE 5

1st and 3rd system phrasing: (slur covers eighth note chord also.)
"Piu mosso" not indicated.
"A la dance" is written here instead.

PAGE 6

"Tranquillo" not in manuscript.

Bar 4: In the original orchestrated manuscript the "and" of beat one
in the bass is a "G", not an "F", but, in the piano manuscript it's
an "F".

Bars 5 and 6: "Deciso" and "scherzando" not given.

Bar 6: **pp** is dynamic given.

Bar 7: Portamentos are added to each fermata; broken chord symbol
not given; poco agitato and poco cresc. not given in Bar 8.

Bars 8–9 and 11–12: Accented
octaves in L.H. on 1st and 3rd
beats.
Phrases extend to second beat
creating a "jazzier" agitato. 3rd
and 4th beats with one phrase.
Page 7, 1st measure the same.
"Agitato" and ⟨ ⟩ are
editor's markings.

Bar 10: Rhythm is easier to read as notated in manuscript.
mf not given.
cresc. not given, Bar 11.

PAGE 7

Bar 2: No *f* given.

Bars 4–5: Some sixteenth notes are notated individually, not
beamed; probably meant to imply "crisper" performance.

Bar 9: *ff* is Gershwin's. "Molto marcato" not in manuscript.

Bars 6, 9, 10 and Bar 1 on Page 8: 1st note in bass (beat 1) are
   played one octave higher.
Bars 7 and 8 have eighth notes on the downbeat. Note phrasing.

PAGE 8

Bar 2: Phrased:

Bar 6: Bars 6, 7 and the 1st beat of Bar 8 are notated as eighth
   notes and eighth rests, but, are written as quarter notes in piano
   manuscript.

PAGE 11

Bar 9: No dynamics given.

PAGE 13

ff for this section. No other dynamics given.

PAGE 15

For Conductor's information:

Bar 1–9 and 1-6 on page 16: Nothing was written for the piano
   part.

Bar 9: "Glissando" is written under Bar 9 (Page 15) and Bars 1-6
   on Page 17. Nothing is indicated in the orchestrated manuscript
   for the piano part.

Editor's suggestion:

Begin glissando on first note of Bars 1–3 and 5–7 and end glissando on quarter note chord.

PAGE 16

Bars 9–10 (page 28): Bars 156–159 this edition for 4 missing orchestra bars.

Bar 12: No chord in manuscript.

PAGE 17

Bar 9 and Bar 1 (Page 18): The example to the right shows Bar 9 (Page 17) and Bar 1 (Page 18) as they exist in the original facsimile edition of the orchestration. The two Bars in the previously printed score and the piano manuscript differ slightly. The editor feels that either version is acceptable.

PAGES 19–20

Page 19: "Meno mosso e poco scherzando" not indicated, only "slower and marked" appears. No staccatos indicated.

Bars 14–15: After Bar 14, the following insert appears which leads to Page 20, Bar 1. Phrase markings, staccatos, accents, etc. are the editor's.

Note: in original manuscript, this section is crossed out but it is undetermined if this was done by Gershwin. When inserted, it forms a continuity compatible with measures 13–15 (Page 19), 5th system, and measures 1–4 (Page 20), 1st system.

This section does not appear in orchestrated manuscript and is the only re-inserted passage that does not appear in both manuscripts.

(page 20)

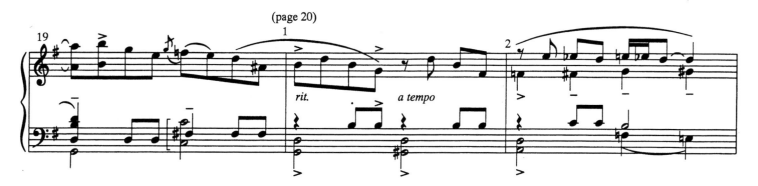

PAGE 20

Bars 5 and 9: No grace notes.

Bars 7–8: Harmonic additions.

PAGE 21

Bars 1–2: Piano and orchestrated manuscript are slightly different.

Bar 7: No grace note.

PAGE 22

Note to the conductor:

Bar 7 leads into the following ten measures, after which Bar 8 comes in.

Accent's are editor's.

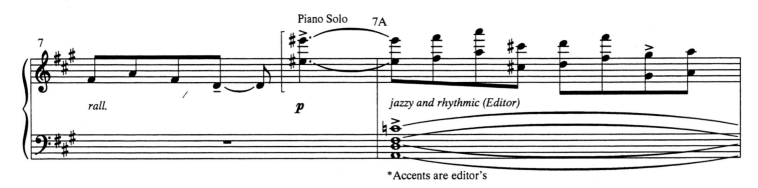

*Accents are editor's

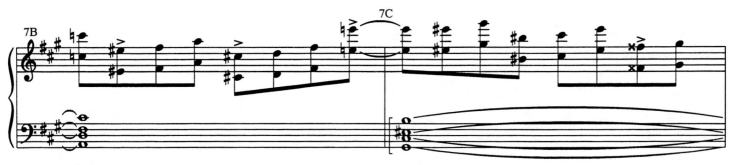

Bar 6: Dynamic's are editor's.

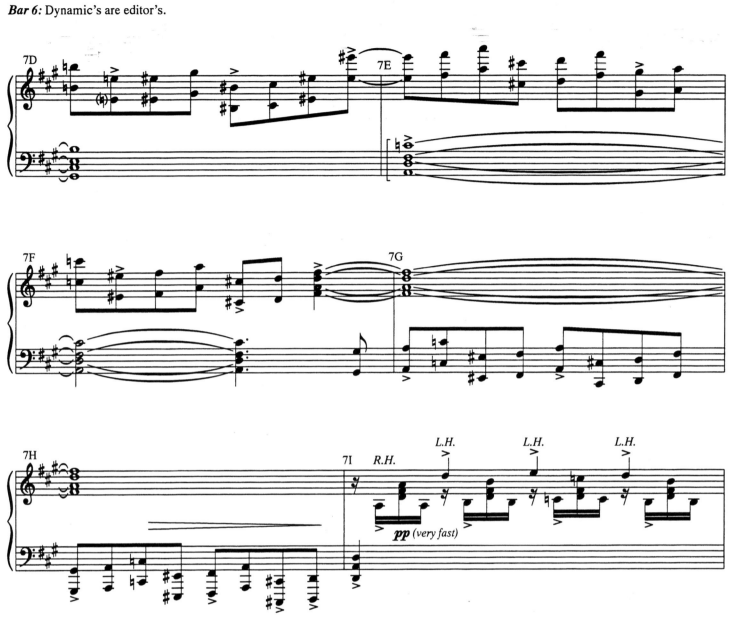

Bar 6: Editor's optional left hand:

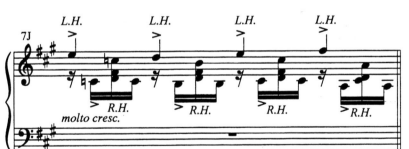

In orchestrated manuscript, L.H. is notated as in Page 23 Bar 2, not
given in piano manuscript.

PAGE 25

Bar 5: Gershwin's words: "Slower and increase".

PAGE 26

No grace notes on 3rd beat for Bars 2, 6, 7, 9, 10 and 13. Bar 7 no
   grace note on 1st beat.

Bar 16 is notated one octave higher. "Octave lower" is then written
   in but it is not proven to be Gershwin's hand. Bar 16 as notated
   appears one octave higher in the original orchestrated manuscript
   as well. Poco rall., portamontos, fermatas, cresc. and decresc. are
   not Gershwin's.

Bars 2 and 6: R.H. chord: no "F".

Bars 3 and 7: R.H. chord: no "C".

On this entire page (26), all chords are written as quarter notes, not
   eighth notes followed by eighth rests, as in previously published
   edition.

PAGE 27

"Agitato" not indicated in Bar 5, nor is "*ff*".

PAGE 27–28

No accents, etc. indicated for Page 27, Bar 13 and Page 28, Bars
   1–3.

PAGE 28

Cadenza: Dynamics are editor's.

There is no C♯ notated. Sixteenth notes appear as beamed groups of
   four.

"Brilliante" is not Gershwin's.

Cadenza is fully notated in piano manuscript and blank in orchestrated manuscript in which the words "wait for nod" appear.

Bar 11: Only "rubato" is written here. No dynamics indicated, nor
   any ritards, for the following four bars.

PAGE 29

"Con espressione" not in piano manuscript, just "Andantino
   moderato".

"Grandioso ma non troppo" not in manuscript, just "a tempo".

PAGE 30

"Lightly" written at piano entrance, not "poco rubato", or
   "leggiero". No staccatos.

PAGE 31–32

Bars 9–11 and Bars 1–7 on Page 32 are notated incorporating two
   measures per phrase. That is, this section was originally com-
   prised of twenty bars instead of ten. In its original state, there
   emerges a new compatibility between this section and the theme
   which follows: Page 32, Bars 10–15 and Bars 18–20 and Page 33,
   (in the L. H.) Bar 1. It appears in both manuscripts and is also
   equal to preceding orchestra-piano dialogue (see following):
   pp is Gershwin's. Fingering and markings are editor's as well as
   suggestion to play this section with a steady but increasing
   tempo.

Also note: Page 32, Bars 10–11, 12–13, 14–15, 18–19, 20, and Page
   33, Bar 1: ascending small notes are editorial suggestions, as only
   the first 3 notes in cue size in Bar 10 are notated in either
   manuscript.

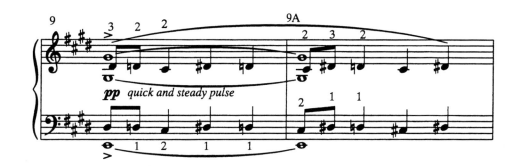

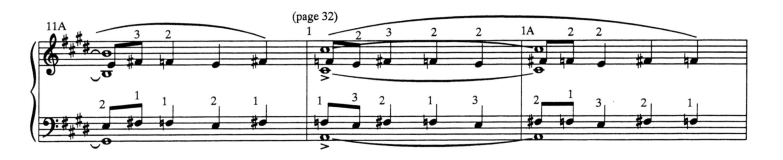

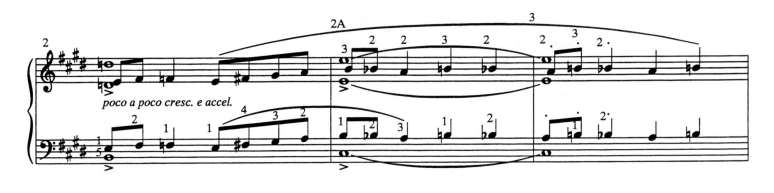

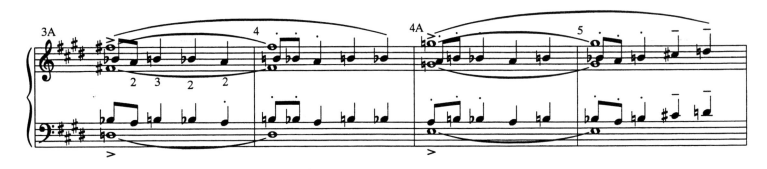

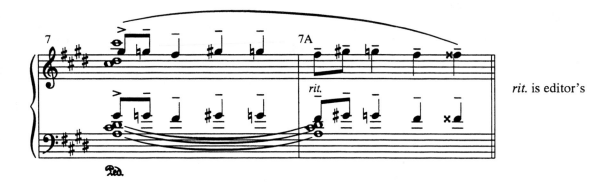

rit. is editor's

PAGE 33

Bar 9: No sixteenth notes in R.H. of beat four.

After Bar 13: The following section appears not only in the original piano manuscript, but also in the original orchestrated manuscript, therefore confirming that it was not intended for deletion. The first four bars are repeated one octave higher in both manuscripts, extending the piano solo.

Note: tremolos extend for three bars in both manuscripts.

Also note: In manuscript, C♮, as indicated here, is notated in bottom staff (*) in both manuscripts, Bar 9 below. The unexpected dissonance of Bars 9 and 10 makes sense when viewed as a concluding statement of the theme with a spartan cleansing ascent.

Bar 14: "Finale" appears here to define this section. No other interpretive clues are given by Gershwin.

Throughout this section (Bar 18, Page 33 through Bar 20, Page 34 and Bars 5–12, Page 35), except for Bar 14, Page 35, no sixteenth notes are beamed (see example above). This is clearly an intentional device by Gershwin to insure visually that the sixteenth notes are played with a hammerlike evenness.

Fermatas in Bars 15 and 17 are editor's.

PAGE 34

Bar 20:
①No fermata is indicated.
②A "G♯" follows the "E" and there is no ritard.

PAGE 35

①The following eight bars appear between bars 4 and 5.
②"*pp*" and tempo are editor's, accents are Gershwin's.

③Note: in original manuscript the C♯ octave is marked "tremolo" for the last two bars.

Last system: (p. 35) Gershwin's words: "Marcato moderato" *not* "Allegio agitato e misterioso" for orchestra's entrance.

PAGE 36

Piano part is notated in piano manuscript beginning at third system.

PAGES 37–40

"Piano unis with orch." is only designation until Bar 7, Page 40 where "Slower" is indicated, not "Grandioso".
"Agitato" section, Page 38, 2nd system: no piano part in either manuscript.

PAGE 40

Bar 1: Octaves in the piano part are editor's. Original manuscript has no music written, except for orchestration where "accelerando" is written, not "molto moderato" as in previously published score.

PAGE 41

Bars 5 and 7: No notation after first eighth note, that is, 32nds (♩♫♫) not in either manuscript.

PAGE 42

Bar 5: First beat: there is no evidence of a 9 note grouping in any
manuscript. "Grandioso" is written over this measure with a *fff*
and is notated for orchestra (piano unis is implied here).

Bar 8: Treble clef 16th and 8th note chords are octaves in
both manuscripts. There is no whole note chord for the
piano (downbeat). A 𝄾 rest is indicated for both hands.

Bar 9: Contains whole note chord marked "tremolo" for the entire
measure (no other chords).

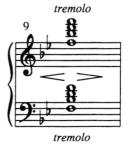

Bar 10: Chords in both manuscripts are different from the previously published edition:
As originally notated:

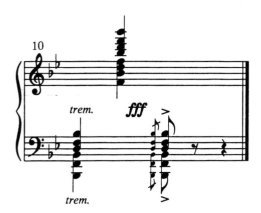

RHAPSODY IN BLUE

January 7, 1924

Music by
GEORGE GERSHWIN

Researched, Restored and Edited by
ALICIA ZIZZO

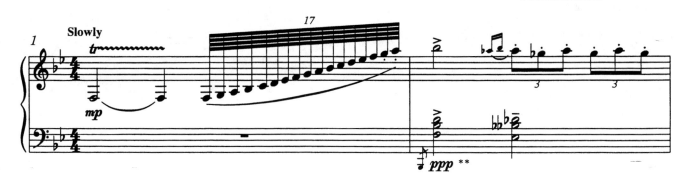

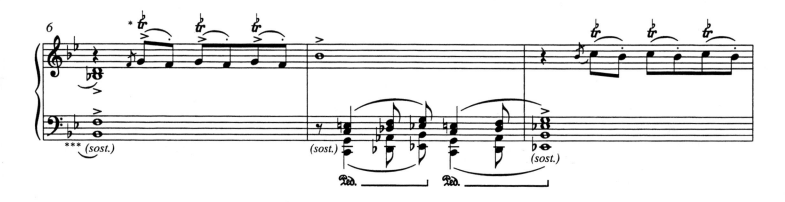

* Phrases, slurs, portamentos, and staccatos this page are Gershwin's, except grace notes bars 6 and 8
 which are editor's suggestion. Originally notated as eighth notes.

** Gershwin's - as in original manuscript.

*** *(sost.)* denotes middle sostenuto pedal. It is important to "catch" only the notes indicated.

* Phrases, accents, slurs this page are Gershwin's except on the last system.
** *f* is Gershwin's.

* The word "chord" is written here in ms.
** "Rit.", accents, phrases and staccatos this page are Gershwin's.

18

* As indicated in original manuscript.
** 2 suggested fingerings, and, by eliminating the A from R.H. chords, passage becomes easier to play.

*All phrases, accents, staccatos, portamentos this page are Gershwin's except phrases in line 4, bar 1
which may facilitate understanding of this measure rhythmically.
**In original orch. ms., there is a "G" instead of an F♮.
***As in manuscript.

* Phrase marks in measures 61–64 show where each of 4 beats fall.
** Phrases and accents in measures 65, 66 and 67 are Gershwin's.
*** The eighth rest must be strictly observed.

* As indicated in original manuscript.
** L.H. cross over is optional but recommended for greater ease of performance.
*** Gershwin plays this bass on piano rolls, differing slightly from original manuscript.

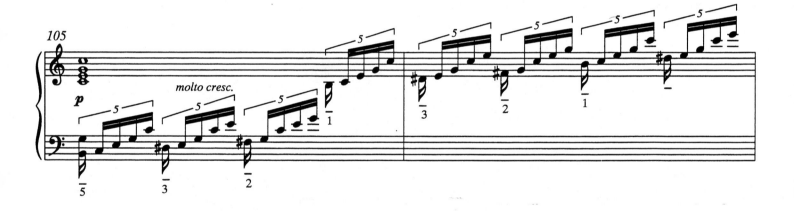

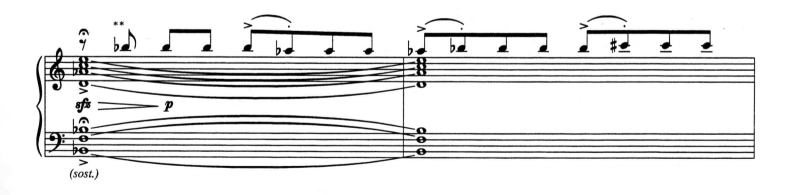

* Optional rhythm in treble clef:

** In original manuscript, no sixteenth notes are indicated, as in previous edition.

* If possible, chords in brackets should not be broken.

25

* As in original orchestrated manuscript.

* Accents this page are Gershwin's.

** Optional:

* This version appears in original orchestrated manuscript. In solo piano manuscript, it appears as found in first published edition.

* Phrasing and accents (>) this section are Gershwin's.
** No grace notes indicated here in manuscript.

*The following four bars appear in piano manuscript, but not in orchestrated manuscript. There are markings in piano manuscript suggesting that Gershwin considered deleting them. They are included here because they form a continuity compatible with measures 12–15 on page 17, (4th and 5th systems) and measures 1–4, on page 18, (1st and 2nd systems).

* The following twelve measures have been reinserted. They appear in both the original piano manuscript and the original orchestrated manuscript.

*Begin slowly and accel.

* As indicated in original manuscript.

* Crossed hands as indicated in original manuscript, and chords are written as quarter notes, no eighth notes.
** No F is indicated in manuscript in these chords as in original published edition.
*** No C is indicated in manuscript in these chords as in original published edition.

* As indicated in original manuscript.

** Grace notes do not appear in original manuscript.

*** In both original manuscripts (orchestra and piano, and piano solo), this measure indicated one octave higher. Also, no *rit.* or fermatas are indicated.

* In both original manuscripts, a "G" is written, not an "F" as the top note. But an "F" is in keeping with the melodic structure.

* In the original manuscript, there is no C♯ written, contrary to previously published editions.

** As indicated in original manuscript. Although doubled in value, the first two measures of this new section are similar rhythmically to the three "rubato" measures that end the preceding section, indicating that Gershwin probably intended a less "dramatic" transition to this famous theme than commonly believed.

*** (sost.): catch only the whole notes with sustaining pedal by releasing other notes quickly (staccato).

40

* As indicated in original manuscript.
** The following 20 measures have been restored according to both original manuscripts.

* The original manuscript is sketchy here and does not contain an "E" in this chord as is present in former editions.

*No sixteenth notes are indicated in the right hand for the and of beat four.

* As indicated in original manuscript. The following ten measures appear in both manuscripts.
Second system repeats one octave higher although not shown here.
** In original manuscript, sixteenth notes are written separately (not beamed), an intentional device by Gershwin to insure separation between notes (almost stacc.).
"Finale" is Gershwin's only directive.

* Ossia: do not tie B.

* In original manuscript, the C♯ octave is marked "tremolo", followed by an additional measure:

This can be included at the discretion of the performer.

** As in original manuscript.

* Ossia: in both original manuscripts, no piano part is given. The orchestra part is offered here as another option.

** Ossia: ***As indicated in original manuscript.

*The downbeat is only notation. No 32nd notes or arpeggiated chords are indicated. Manuscript. is sketchy here.

** Original manuscript.

***This ending is the only one indicated in both original manuscripts. In first bar, last system, all treble chords after whole note are written as octaves in manuscript. Bass is as shown.

ALICIA ZIZZO

Alicia Zizzo's gifts as a pianist were recognized early in her career by the legendary Dimitri Mitropolus. After her Carnegie Hall recital debut at the age of eleven, Mitropolus referred to her as "an extraordinary talent...with a musical perception which is not often heard."

As a child prodigy, she became the pupil of Dr. Carlos Buhler. Following in the tradition of his own great teachers, Alfred Cartot and Ferruccio Busoni, Dr. Buhler trained Alicia to play in the refined style of those venerable masters.

Alicia has appeared as a featured performer in many of the major centers of music in the United States. She has also been a featured artist on television and radio in New York. Her great talent eventually brought her to the concert stages of London, Amsterdam, Vienna, Budapest, Warsaw, Edinburgh, Glasgow and Germany.

Today, Alicia's scholarly commitment is in the research and restoration of the classical piano literature of George Gershwin. Her goal is to enhance Gershwin's remarkably small classical piano solo repertoire. Working with the Library of Congress and with leading Gershwin scholar, Edward Jablonski, she has spent the last several years investigating the composer's original classical piano manuscripts and their differences from the published printed works.

Ms. Zizzo's objective with Gershwin's manuscripts is not to make just another arrangement of his melodies but to literally reconstruct, from fragments, sketches, partially complete scores and his own manuscripts, brand new compositions. Her reconstructions never lose sight of the purity and intent of his original creation.

In collaboration with Warner Bros. Publications, she has begun these restorations. They include a piano solo based on Gershwin's string composition, "Lullaby," a piano suite of his 1922 opera *Blue Monday, The Complete Preludes* (including the unpublished ones) and a brand new edition, *The Annotated Rhapsody In Blue*. She is currently working on some miniature versions of other Gershwin compositions.

All this is being accomplished with the help of Warner Bros. Publications, the cooperation of the Gershwin estate, and the blessing of George's sister, Frances.

All of the Gershwin/Zizzo editions have been recorded by the Carlton Classics label on two CDs: *Gershwin Rediscovered Vols. 1 & 2*. Ms. Zizzo's work on Gershwin has been acclaimed on four continents and in major radio and television venues as well as in many news publications throughout the world. Her work in this field has been welcomed and praised as an important contribution to American music.